NFT for Be

C000099801

The Ultimate Guide to Non-Fungible Tokens

(Digital Art, Crypto and Collectibles)

By

Andrew Johnston

Table of Contents

Introduction

Within the fruitful fields of innovation, technological advancements trigger subsequent opportunities for the installation of a market in which the originators of new technological products can exchange what is truly the culmination of years of work and research for the gratification and sustainment of the all-mighty dollar. Within the last twenty years, the focus of global technological advancement has been on the digitalization of business practice. Once constrained to on-premise systems and archaic computers, the age of digital computing has ushered in more flexibility and agility to the fast-paced business environment. The advent of the digital age has also destroyed the barriers that once constrained society. Barriers of distance have been destroyed and bridges of globalization constructed in their place. While the barriers of accessibility have been among the greatest changes from the age of digitalization, perhaps the greatest barrier that has been destroyed has been the barrier to wealth that once gave credence to the phrase "starving artist." Whereas there was an impending doom that shrouded the success of artists around the world, removing the barrier of accessibility has created a market for their digital goods, a path to success now outlined and a new-found appreciation for their art suddenly turning valueless works of art into multi-million dollar purchases. While the entire realm of digital art has benefited tremendously from the age of digitalization, a new market that has been the recipient of the age of digitalization is known as the NFT market. The opposite of fungible tokens, non-fungible tokens have taken the digital market by storm, with some works of art selling for as high as $65 million. Even as the sale of this digital art has turned starving artists into affluent artists, the full effect of the NFT market has yet to be seen. To begin, it is helpful to bear in mind the history that made this new digital token market come alive.

The History of Non-Fungible Tokens

When examining the market, any economist or person would recognize that a market exists where an exchange of value is created. For instance, any good, which can be referred to as an asset, will not trade hands unless an equally valuable asset is returned (barring outside interference of course). With this in mind, it is simply seen that for an asset to exist, this asset must be unique. The laws of supply and demand reiterate that the scarcity of a certain asset will create an inverse relationship between quantity demanded and price; however, objects with no scarcity are often regarded as worthless. Assets with no scarcity are regarded as anything but unique and therefore have no value to society and are unable to be purchased. Furthermore, these assets often have no ownership since an asset of no value is unable to be purchased. All of this goes to prove that for an exchange of value to take place, an asset must have an owner and for an asset to have an owner, there must be some minimum value attached to that asset. Neither is able to exist without the other.

With an understanding of the market, it is easy to see how the realm of digital art was for so long, considered a worthless or at the very least, a thankless market. While digital art was beautiful and able to be appreciated by many, it was unable to be transferred in many instances due to its ease of replication (unlimited scarcity) and lack of ownership (lack of value). It would also be advantageous to point out that there is a difference between simple digital art and the topic of this guide, non-fungible tokens. While digital art can be protected by a copyright or trademark, non-fungible tokens are representative of a digital asset that is completely unique. To gain a better understanding of non-fungible tokens, it would be helpful to understand what fungible tokens are. The idea of tokens will be examined later when the invention of blockchain or cryptocurrency is examined but for now, it can be helpful to think of a fungible token as being similar to a common bitcoin. Even as the price of a bitcoin can vary based on its performance within the cryptocurrency market, there is nothing to differentiate one bitcoin from another. If two people were two trade an equal number of bitcoins, they would be in the same fiscal position prior to and after the trade. This is different from non-fungible tokens in that no two non-fungible tokens are alike. Even items of equal perception will be different in some respect. Doing this allows for two important elements of a market: ownership and value. By creating a completely unique asset, the requirements of a perfectly scarce asset are created and the value of the scarce asset will now be the result of agreement between the seller and the buyer. This also fulfills another requirement of a market: ownership. By creating a unique asset, there is always only one owner of the unique asset. While copies of this asset may be seen and the asset is free to be distributed throughout the digital universe, there is truly only one owner of this digital asset and all proceeds of this digital asset will be driven towards that owner unless otherwise stipulated in the agreement. This brings up the crux of non-fungible tokens: the advent of blockchain. Without blockchain, the world of non-fungible tokens would not exist; however, without blockchain, neither would the market of cryptocurrency. With this in mind, it would be helpful to take a closer look at the history and origin of blockchain.

The History of Blockchain

The history of blockchain is almost as secure as the security produced by its presence. This is proven by the fact that to date, the originator of blockchain is still unknown. Blockchain was first given status as an idea as far back as 1982 when David Chaum, a cryptographer, demonstrated the security and potential market to be created by a "blockchain-esque" system. The idea was presented in his dissertation, entitled "Computer Systems Established, Maintained, and Trusted by Mutually Suspicious Groups." Chaum's dissertation caused significant ripples among the cryptography industry, with many asserting that blockchain was the future of network security. There was simply no market, however, as the personal computer had yet to be delivered on a mass scale and the only individuals who respected such an idea were nerdy computer scientists. Nearly ten years later, this idea of security being feasible through a chain of blocks was visited once again by Stuart Haber and W. Scott Stornetta. In a complimentary piece, these authors produced another aspect of blockchain that would be integral in its future development: the security of a date stamp. Essentially, while Chaum had proposed that security could be implemented by means of developing a series of blocks, Haber and Stornetta came along and asserted that further security could be derived by making the date stamp on these blocks of data unchangeable. Out of the three cryptographers, Haber and Stornetta would be the closest to developing what is now known as blockchain. One year after publishing their assertions, the duo formulated the first of these unchangeable data stamps using a security feature known as Merkle Trees. Merkle Trees were first invented in 1979 by Ralph Merkle and would lay the foundation for the eventual discovery of blockchain. Within Merkle Trees, a series of nodes are coupled together, each beating a different numbered hash that identifies the node with the parent node. While security was a large breakthrough with Haber and Stornetta's development of the Merkle Trees, an additional development was the ability to store large amounts of data in these "boxes" of data.

For the next few years, little attention would be paid to cryptography and to the concept of blockchain. However, as alluded to previously, an unknown source would eventually formulate the development of blockchain, taking his predecessors' work to fruition and creating the secure and tamper-proof blockchain that is known today. The concept and title of blockchain was first introduced by an entity named Satoshi Nakamoto; however, to date it is not known whether Nakamoto is a real person or simply a group of people or a false name. While this has added to the mystery of blockchain and the overall suspicion people have of the cryptographic industry, it has led to a greater sense of trust in the industry, due to the fact that no one entity is regulating it. Rather, an unknown source created the blockchain and now anyone can use this development.

After the first blockchain was developed by Nakamoto, the concept was driven further by subsequent developments, drawing from the original creation of the Merkle Trees and adding a key element of blockchain: automatic development and record-keeping. With homage to the Merkle Trees, Nakamoto gave the blocks autonomy by removing the requirement that they be verified and signed by an individual. Now, the blockchains were outfitted with their own record book known as the ledger, a ledger upon which the names of all known owners was recorded and a leader that recorded every transaction to which that the blockchain was exposed. Nearly six years after the first introduction of blockchain, the network reached a total data usage of 20 gigabytes—hardly indicative of the growing storm that blockchain was creating. Only one year later, that file size had grown by 50%, showing the rapid ascent and acceptance of the cryptography industry. After an additional year, the network data size grew nearly 67% to 50 gigabytes and only one year after that, the file size doubled. Today, the size of the file is estimated to be in excess of 200 gigabytes, each piece of data recording the ownership and transaction details of every usage of blockchain.

It is important to note that the concept of blockchain might have been conceptualized in the 1970s and developed in the 2000s; however, the name blockchain was not adopted until early 2016. It was during this same year that blockchain began to take off as a feasible means of securing digital content and exchanges; however, its growth among corporate business was still quite slow with a mere 1% of Chief Information Officers surveyed by Gartner in 2018 revealing that they had adopted the security of blockchain. Additionally, its future does not seem to be within corporate business as only 8% of these surveyed chief information officers expressed any plans to begin adopting the edicts of blockchain. Nonetheless, blockchain has found its success in the world of cryptography and the financial ties of the blockchain movement seem to have it nestled firmly within the digital environment.

How Blockchain Works

With an understanding of how blockchain was invented, it is also necessary to consider how a blockchain works. The security capabilities of a single blockchain are quite impressive and when understood, give the reader a sense of the future this invention has within the digital environment. True to its name, blockchain is comprised of numerous blocks that are not centralized and are filled with the data of every single transaction of which that blockchain has been a part. A popular example of blockchain's capabilities is found in cryptocurrencies where each cryptocurrency is secured by blockchain. When a singular asset of cryptocurrency is traded or altered, this data is recorded within the blockchain structure attached to the cryptocurrency and is secured, meaning that no individuals can edit this blockchain unless all future blocks within this blockchain are also edited. This perfectly exemplifies the "general ledger" assertions and descriptions of blockchain, showing how the blockchain is able to gather large amounts of data. Additionally, whenever a blockchain is attached to an asset that is pertinent to an individual, they are able to manually verify this asset's validity using the data of the blockchain. Every single transaction will be recorded in this blockchain and will therefore be able to be compared with the records submitted by the owner—giving the buyer or analyst an undeniable source of truth for the blockchain. Additionally, this helps secure the validity of an asset by warding off attempts to "spend" an asset twice. This ensures that an asset is not sold but then used by the original owner again. This will be examined in greater detail when the creation of non-fungible tokens is revealed but it is also worth noting that this general ledger of blockchain is also helpful in allowing for the unlimited distribution of digital assets while retaining a single owner. Essentially, one could think of this concept as countless individuals downloading a single photo from the internet while one individual remains the sole owner of the photograph.

In addition, to replicating and creating additional blocks per transaction, a singular blockchain resembles an onion in which multiple layers are peeled back to reveal a subsequent layer. These layers include the infrastructure of the blockchain, the networking (peer-to-peer network), a consensus (the validation of the blockchain), the data (the individual blocks of data), and any applications that are connected to the blockchain. With each block forming after additional data becomes available, these blocks form their chain, tracing their lineage to the original block that was created upon the birth of the digital asset, referred to as the genesis block. It is also worth noting that a single blockchain does not necessarily resemble a single-file line of blocks but in some cases can have instances in which two blocks are created at the same time. In instances such as this, the block with the higher value will be retained as the block upon which future blocks will be created. This instance is exemplified in the instance of bitcoin where a single bitcoin will use a security measure known as the proof of work system in which the segment of the fork with the greatest value in work will be retained as the chain upon which future blocks will be built. By doing this, creation of dual chains within one blockchain are mitigated and minimized to instances of no more than two per fork.

There is an important exception to the instances of a fork in the creation of blocks. When the program of a blockchain is updated and new software is introduced, a fork will take place so that the old software is recognizable as being at its end of life while the new software can be traced back to the earliest block of its introduction. In instances where some of the nodes refuse to update software and continue with the old software, a condition known as a permanent split will occur and the software will be permanently split at the hard fork. One of the greatest examples of this hard fork occurred with the grandfather of blockchain deviants, Ethereum. When a group of hackers attempted to update the code of Ethereum, the blockchain hard forked, resulting in two chains: Ethereum and Ethereum Classic. In a follow up example, a disagreement centering on how often the transactions for bitcoin should take place, a hard fork was reached resulting in the creation of Bitcoin and Bitcoin Cash.

Another important aspect of blockchain is the time needed to create the actual blocks. The frequency of creation for new blocks is dependent on how each blockchain is programmed within its infrastructure but some blockchains will update as quickly as every five seconds while other well-known blockchains use a timer of nearly ten minutes. In creating new blocks autonomously, the most gratifying and attractive element of blockchain becomes apparent: its ability to be decentralized and not controlled by a single regulator. This is primarily due to the storage of data within the peer-to-peer network. Whereas a computer network has a single access point that is the hotspot that hackers pinpoint and use to gain access to the entire system, the decentralized element of blockchain makes it much harder to penetrate. Not only does this decentralization protect blockchain from outside attacks: it also protects it from inside attacks with no one point being able to cause failure for the entire system. Going further, the data that is stored within each block of a blockchain is considered to be extremely safe and unable to be deleted or edited, giving a new level of security to data that is not attainable under other systems.

Just from this brief history and explanation of the functionality of blockchain, one can see how attractive this opportunity was for the digital media crowd. Whereas in the past, digital media had been exploited by a lack of protection and the seemingly impossible task of protecting an original while displaying it for the world to see, blockchain now gave digital artists hope that their digital art would be protected and their livelihoods restored.

The Creation of Non-Fungible Tokens

Whereas the history of blockchain is far more robust and dates back to the invention of the computer, the creation and use of non-fungible tokens is relegated primarily to post-2010 work and is ambiguous at best. In 2012, the first non-fungible tokens were created when Yoni Hesse used his personal blog to formulate the suggestion that new tokens for Bitcoin needed to be made. In essence, cryptographers had been grappling with the idea of how they could arrange for asset transfer while using the Bitcoin blockchain. One of the tenants of marketing is the easy transfer of ownership and transferring Bitcoins was anything but easy. Additionally, Hesse formulated that by creating a token of sorts, the reach of Bitcoin would be extended to tangible elements as well. With tokens, Bitcoin blockchain could represent real estate, stocks, commodities, and fiat currencies in addition to giving representation to other cryptocurrencies as well. After Hesse's blog, concepts began to swirl and numerous suggestions were put forth, none greater than Meni Rosenfield who composed a white paper that gave the instructions for creating a token for Bitcoin, the Colored Coins. As the white paper made its way around the internet, its work captivated the attention of many who read it. While the paper was not able to show a complete way of creating the colored coin, it left the attempts to those who read it, offering inspiration instead of instruction and direction instead of dictate. The white paper clearly laid out why colored coins were needed: to offer more than simple transactions of Bitcoin to the cryptographic environment. Colored Coins, though still only an idea, would give developers the chance to create a cryptographic representation of a fungible or tangible item drastically opened the cryptographic market.

Only one year later, crypto would see the fruition of this paper with the creation of the first protocol for Bitcoin, the Colored Coin Protocol. Even as the Colored Coin Protocol gave foundation for the creation of Colored Coins, it would take another year for instructions on how developers could create Colored Coins. This came through the EPOBC Protocol release from Chromaway. The process of years of research and postulation, Colored Coins first became available to the public in 2015 and greatly laid the foundation for the future non-fungible tokens that would come about later. Andrew Steinwold reveals that the following can be represented by Colored Coins: "property, coupons, other cryptocurrencies, shares of a company, subscriptions, access tokens, digital collectables." The last part of his list (though not exhaustive) is quite interesting since it reveals the first time that individuals considered digital collectables being worth protecting; however, that will be discussed in greater length later in the paper.

While Colored Coins showed how far the world of cryptography had transcended in the past decade, it faced a major barrier due to one thing: individual perception. What made Bitcoin so relevant is that people agreed on its value. And those who didn't simply did not participate in its transactions, causing the price to diminish, while those who did, used it extensively, causing its price to go up. It was different with Colored Coins, however; the value of an asset, tangible or intangible, could not be scripted with Colored Coins if the two parties did not agree on that asset's worth. Thus, Colored Coins truly failed to gain traction in the world of

13

cryptography and simply proved itself as a framework that would be vital in the future implementation of the non-fungible tokens.

Whereas Colored Coins solved many problems of the cryptographic industry but continued to make problems by essentially requiring a consensus for use, it failed fast enough for individuals to scrap it for its best parts. It is important to note that Colored Coins still exist today. They may not be used extensively but they are still in existence. Greater than their existence is their inspiration, however, and that went on full display in 2014 with the introduction of the next greatest use of blockchain: Counterparty.

An Introduction to Counterparty

Drawing from the success of blockchain on the peer-to-peer network, the introduction of Counterparty in 2014 gave developers another open-source protocol that used blockchain as its engine. While Counterparty allows the trade of most cryptocurrencies such as Bitcoin, Ether, Ripple, and its predecessor Colored Coins, it also has an organic currency known as XCP, which was created in unique fashion.

In early 2014, developers Robert Dermody, Adam Krellenstein, and Evan Wagner pooled financial and cognitive resources to create Counterparty. The platform was essentially designed to give its users the ability to trade cryptocurrencies, opening the market for the sale of goods and services with cryptocurrency as the means of payment. When issuing its XCP currency, the founders of Counterparty opted to create the currency using a funding mechanism known as a proof of burn. In doing this, the founders intentionally delivered 2125.63 Bitcoins to an address that was known to be inaccessible, ensuring that the coins would never be accessed again and therefore giving the platform a foundation that would distribute equal opportunity and wealth to its users. This followed the pattern of giving the power to the users instead of having a single centralized source to regulate the value of bitcoins or the other cryptocurrencies.

One of the fundamental aspects of Counterparty was the ability of the users to create assets. In doing so, there are two types of assets that can be created.

The first type of asset is the Named asset. This asset is named using alphabetical entities and the stringed name can vary from 4-12 characters. Of interest, the only two assets that were allowed to have three-letter names were BTC (Bitcoin) and XCP (Counterparty's currency). For those who desire to use a different style of asset naming, there is also the numeric asset. Within this asset, the asset is named by affixing a prefix A and then an integer. Once the asset is named, there are other aspects that also must be delineated. To ensure security, it is important that the asset contain information about the source of the issuance. Additionally, the quantity being issued is also very important and a final piece of information required for issuance is the description of the asset. After the asset is created, the asset can be placed on the market or directly sent to a recipient. To be sent, there are additional pieces of information that must be filled out. The issuer must outline the source of the asset (where the asset originated and who the owner is), the quantity of the asset to be delivered, and the destination to which the asset is to be delivered. Today, many of the use-cases for Counterparty are found in betting, tickets, Token Controlled Access points, Programmable Smart Contracts, and derivatives to name a few. As the Counterparty community matured, other instances of use included a meme trading function and the issuance of trading cards.

As Counterparty continued to give individual investors access to cryptocurrency like never before, there was another access that was being created: the initial coin offering. To gain an understanding of how important this was for non-fungible tokens, it would be helpful to take a closer look at the first initial coin offering to ever be presented: the Spells of Genesis initial coin offering.

An Introduction to Spells of Genesis

Until this point in the history of blockchain and specifically cryptocurrencies, its primary use had been the facilitating of representing assets in a digital environment. Spells of Genesis sought to change this, however, and by their own declaration, became "the first blockchain-based mobile game ever made." Drawing on the addictive traits of collection and the already-existent token trading available through blockchain, Spells of Genesis sought to drive their mobile platform through the blockchain engine while using a well-known feature of blockchain: trading card games. In this mobile game, which is still available, players are able to collect cards, seeking to collect cards that are able to be combined to create a powerful deck of cards. In doing so, players are able to "wage war" with their opponents. The cards, affectionately known as "orbs" are designed from a background in fantasy and are able to be purchased for collection. The Spells of Genesis represented the first time a mobile game had been created on the blockchain engine and also showed yet another way that blockchain had found a means of monetizing its existence.

While proponents of cryptocurrency were quick to adopt the gamification of the cryptographic world, there was another feature that differentiated Spells of Genesis from other contributes. To provide context, most anyone would recognize that to release a new stock, companies hire a financial institution to underwrite the investment and offer the newly released shares to the public or private investors by means of an initial public offering.

Doing so allows the financial institution to control the supply and demand of the new offering while also setting a starting price for the stock. Additionally, these initial public offerings, also known as IPOs, are usually only available to a select number of investors who are willing to purchase large amounts of the stock and therefore push the price towards a higher valuation. Within the cryptocurrency industry, new coins were being introduced on markets such as Counterparty but the lack of hype around a new currency being released led many to believe there was great potential for even more cryptocurrency to be purchased. With this in mind, the creators of Spells of Genesis set out to pioneer a new form of introducing cryptocurrency to the market: the initial coin offering, otherwise known as the ICO. Following in the desires of the creators of Bitcoin, the initial coin offerings have largely remained unregulated, differing substantially form the rival IPO. According to leading investment firms, an initial coin offering is available to most anyone as long as they are able to produce and distribute the cryptocurrency. To create an initial coin offering, all one has to do is compose a white paper explaining the workings of the new cryptocurrency, market the coin via a website or application, and then support the new cryptocurrency with investors and funding.

With Spells of Genesis introducing the world of cryptocurrency to the ICO, the game had officially changed for cryptography. Access that had already been relatively open was now more open than ever before and the hype of cryptocurrency exploded. In their ICO, Spells of Genesis released a cryptocurrency called BitCrystals, which is still used today as the primary source of funding for the company and the sole source of tokenization to play the game. Since the introduction of the ICO in 2015, the pool of available cryptocurrencies has risen to nearly 4,000, an explosion of growth that is likely to continue given the hype of major cryptocurrencies such as Ethereum and Bitcoin.

As can be seen by the non-linear progression of cryptocurrencies, the world of cryptography is one of genius and tremendous imagination. If one could imagine a use of digital currency, there were likely others who would also share that desire and support the creation, financially. As is yet to be seen though, the world of cryptography has only recently exploded. Even as the creation of the marketplaces for trading cryptocurrencies was slowly evolving, these were merely creating the foundation that would one day lead to the most explosive use of blockchain yet: the NFT.

In 2016, Counterparty took their development of the cryptographic industry to a new level when they began issuing well-known trading cards on their marketplace. The most well-known of these cards was the Force of Will. While the presence of Force of Will on the Counterparty platform only added to the prestige of the network, the import of Force of Will to the platform also showed that individuals with no prior knowledge or even exposure to cryptocurrency were starting to grow interested in the platform. Until now, most of the users of cryptocurrency had been those with a background in digital media or computer science. Now, however, the world of trading cards was starting to become interested in the lower-priced alternatives to the tangible cards they had so long traded. Following in the footsteps of Force of Will was something far greater however: the meme dictionary of Rare Pepe.

The Development of Rare Pepe

To understand how important Rare Pepe was to the world of cryptocurrency, one would need to go back to the early 2000s when Matt Furie created what he thought would be a simple comic called *Boy's Club*. One of the characters in *Boy's Club* was a green frog that also possessed a humanoid body. Due to the frog's ludicrous sayings and the expressions on its face, its existence soon became legendary. The advent of social media was key to the frog's success as platforms such as Myspace were popular spots for Furie to post his comic strips of Pepe the Frog. In the original drawings, Pepe the Frog was popularized as a frog in the process of urinating with the adopted catch phrase "Feels good man." Additionally, Pepe the Frog was known for shouting "reee" when angered. What drew so many individuals to Pepe the Frog was the ability to have a joke that not everyone knew about. Since Pepe the Frog was constrained to Myspace in its early existence and later solely on 4chan, many considered Pepe the Frog the ultimate inside joke, only drawing more curious fans and therefore driving up its popularity. Pepe the Frog reached stardom in 2014 when celebrities began sharing his image on their personal social media accounts. Most notably, Katie Perry and Nicki Minaj were quick to show their support for Pepe. The increased popularity of Pepe the Frog led to individuals creating their own Pepe masterpieces, transforming the image of the frog into the likeness of celebrities such as Donald Trump and Tiger Woods. As a result of the proliferation of the Pepe memes, some individuals began keeping track of the Pepe memes, ranking them and noting the Rare Pepes that were inherently worth more.

The hype of the Rare Pepe movement reached new heights when they began to be auctioned on eBay and sold on Craigslist. The Pepe fan club successfully pushed the meme to becoming the most popular meme on Twitter while also reaching the top five most important memes in the world. Drawing on previous appearances of his likeness in the Pepe meme, Donald Trump used the memes during his 2016 presidential run. As future President Trump continued to use the meme, rumors of the memes' representation of a racist group began to emanate from outside of the Rare Pepe fanbase. One group, the Anti-Defamation League, went so far as to announce that the images of Rare Pepe were actually considered hate symbols and were tied to an anti-Semitic movement. When Furie, the creator of Pepe the Frog, was asked about the apparent connection between his lovable character and hate speech movements, he replied, "It sucks but I can't control it more than anyone can control frogs on the internet." While Pepe the Frog would eventually be removed from the Boy's Club comic strip, it continues to live on today as one of the greatest memes ever created.

In all truth, Pepe the Frog did not become the greatest meme by social media, however. Its rise to fame beyond an internet meme was thanks to the efforts of monetizing its existence through listing rare editions of the comic, known as Rare Pepe on Counterparty. The first Rare Pepe memes were added to the Counterparty market in late 2016 with individuals taking courses and becoming certified as "experts" in the field of judging the rarity of a select Rare Pepe meme. Going beyond Counterparty, Rare Pepe now exists on its own website with a singular Rare Pepe Meme Directory showing the age and value of the memes. Today, Rare Pepe continues to be traded on cryptocurrency marketplaces, driving up its value.

In looking at the rise of Rare Pepe, no glimpse would be complete without paying homage to a cryptocurrency that was highly instrumental in the meme's rise: Ethereum. In 2017, as the cryptocurrency began to rival the likes of Bitcoin, individuals began trading Rare Pepes using Ethereum and the prospect of creating a trading card that had no shelf life or expiration date quickly pushed developers to focus on the Ethereum market. To show the dynamics of this transition, it is worth paying a closer visit to the origin and rise of Ethereum.

The Introduction of Ethereum

Mentioned earlier, one of the primary means of issuing new cryptocurrency is the creation of a white paper explaining the functionality and creation of the currency. That is precisely what Vitalik Buterin did in 2013 with his proposal for the creation of a new cryptocurrency named Ethereum. Drawing on the success of Bitcoin, Buterin proposed that the currency be as deregulated and decentralized as possible. Of interest, Buterin was actually one of the authors who helped with the formation of Colored Coins in 2013. During the final days before the launch of Colored Coins, Buterin got into a hostile argument with Assia from eToro on how the coins should be reproduced, leading to the split of their work and the birth of Ethereum.

At the time of Buterin's introduction of Ethereum, cryptocurrency had yet to truly begin representing assets with cryptocurrency. Thus far, most of the transactions on the cryptocurrency market had been used to simply transfer funds, not represent tangible or intangible assets such as stocks and real estate. Ethereum was first released to the public in 2015 under the codename Project Frontier. Since that date, there have been twelve releases and Ethereum boasts of a blockchain that is comprised of over 12,244,000 blocks. Ethereum was one of the first cryptocurrencies to pilot the use of miners to secure the validity of the growing blockchain. These miners are simply individuals who have supercomputers and are able to match new transactions with existing blockchain data to prevent the risk of double spending. To understand double spending, it is helpful to consider the mitigation of that within the American dollar. Whereas an individual could not spend a $5 bill in two locations at once, it is much harder to mitigate such a risk in a cryptographic environment where there is potentially the opportunity for someone to trade a cryptocurrency on the market and then use it quickly for another transaction before the individual who purchased the cryptocurrency can spend it.

To mitigate the ability of individuals to double spend their Ether (the currency of Ethereum), miners use their supercomputers (also known as nodes) to validate the chain of code within that specific blockchain before adding the validated block to the blockchain. In doing this, miners are paid a fee for their service. This practice is replicated in Bitcoin where the individuals are paid in Bitcoin. In 2017, the two entities Ethereum and Rare Pepes met with the introduction of the meme marketplace named Peperium. Within this marketplace, individuals were able to create Rare Pepe memes that were fueled by Ethereum and therefore would never be destroyed.

With the introduction of Ethereum-based Rare Pepe memes in 2017, something important overtook the cryptographic industry: the first non-fungible tokens were beginning to show up on the market. Thus far, most of the cryptographic industry had focused on the creation of cryptocurrencies or means of representing assets by cryptocurrencies. Now, individuals were focused on seeking true digital assets that were secured with cryptocurrency but not comprised of cryptocurrency. This would become a reality with the next and most important step of the NFT history: the introduction of CryptoPunks.

The Development of CryptoPunks

In 2017, developers John Watkinson and Matt Hall developed a character generator that produced pixelated characters with unique variables. Over the next two months, the duo would spend all of their time creating unique characters and developing an impressive portfolio. At the time of their creation, CryptoArt was a brand new experience for the cryptographic industry. With the developments of the blockchain security, individuals were more certain that they were the sole owner of the crypto art leading to an explosion of unique artistry around the industry. Watkinson and Hall were among the first to introduce both the art and the monetization of this form of artistry with their project, a project they had affectionally named CryptoPunks as homage to the CyberPunks from the early 90s. When completed, the portfolio of CryptoPunks was comprised of 10,000 "punks," all of which were unique characters that were fueled and secured by the Ethereum security. When examining the portfolio of CryptoPunks, one would be hard pressed to find any common features apart from the pixelation. The characters ranged from celebrity likeness to aliens and animals. What made these characters even more unique was that they were truly generated by a computer. While Watkinson and Hall may have had a hand in setting parameters for the computer program to be confined to, the computer program took care of generating the unique traits of each of the images.

Once completed, the duo introduced their punks to the crypto art world, where Ethereum-loyalists purchased the punks for less than $1 USD each. At first, the launch did not take off and less than .3% of the punks were even purchased. Then, journalism took over. Editors at the media-focused magazine *Mashable* found the CryptoPunks to be exactly what the non-technical mind could understand. Perhaps one did not grasp what the cryptocurrency market was comprised of but who wouldn't like to own a pixelated CryptoPunk? Going further, there were two elements of the CryptoPunk characters that espoused them to the cryptocurrency movement. First, the CyberPunks were scarce. Not only were no two CryptoPunks alike, there were also only 10,000 within the portfolio. Second, the CryptoPunks were secure. Scarcity is only preservable if the owners are ensured they have sole ownership of the asset, digital or tangible. With Ethereum comprising the organs of the CryptoPunks, individuals could rest assured that their punk was owned solely by that individual. With Mashable's story taking the internet by storm, the CryptoPunks sold out quickly. And then began an event that only takes place when scarcity meets a shortage, regulated or unregulated: appreciation of value.

With the final CryptoPunk sold, every punk began an upward trek towards higher valuation, a journey that many aspired would only grow. While these punks are less than five years old, they have created millionaires out of individuals who purchased multiples of them while also making other individuals look like fools for selling the punks so quickly. One instance of this occurred when an individual claimed to have ownership in excess of 1,000 punks. At first, the market for punks appreciated, but very slowly. There was little growth, partially due to the fact that the crypto art industry was still less popular than the cryptocurrency industry. When the CryptoPunks were first introduced to the cryptographic world, the valuation of one Bitcoin stood at just over $1,000. By the middle of December in the same year, that valuation had rocketed to over $18,000. With this in mind, individuals were far more interested in the rapid growth of the Bitcoin than the newly formed crypto art world; however, Bitcoin took the spotlight away from the CryptoPunks but it would soon give the spotlight right back.

The Growth of CryptoPunks

In the latter months of 2017, Bitcoin began to depreciate from its all-time high just days earlier. What had been a steady slope to the top over the past year was a far more volatile ride back to the bottom, taking investors on a lurching trip that would plummet before making a momentary spike before once again plummeting. It is important to remember that this was the first time that a cryptocurrency began appreciating so quickly. For the first time, cryptocurrency was being looked at by retail and institutional investors, not simply the computer geeks who were smart enough to understand the concepts of blockchain. Also, individuals were not looking at cryptocurrency as a means of representing wealth, they were now looking at cryptocurrency as a means of growing wealth. However, it would still be a few years before cryptocurrency began its historical trek upward in 2020-2021. In the meantime, the downfall of Bitcoin set off greater levels of interest in other cryptographic entities, such as crypto art. The timing was perfect for CryptoPunks that had spent the last year appreciating slowly but nonetheless showing the world that an asset could grow in value while doing nothing different other than existing as a scarce resource. Shortly after the downfall of Bitcoin, the valuation of each CryptoPunk began to grow more quickly. Referenced earlier, the individual who had purchased more than 1,000 punks sold the punks in the days shortly before the CryptoPunks began their rapid ascent, leaving what would eventually be worth millions of dollars on the table.

Today, there are some CryptoPunks worth millions of dollars each while others are worth tens of thousands of dollars. Just as the Rare Pepe meme dictionary had individuals dedicated to determining how rare a meme was and estimating value based on those variables, those familiar with the CryptoPunks on a level more intimate than simply purchased value have attributed this difference in valuation to the "aesthetic differences of the punks." In an article for *TechCrunch,* Lucas Matney issued what he considered to be the different variables of punks that lead to the myriad of valuations. "Things aren't always predictable," begins Matney. "Earrings are the most common attribute for punks, commanding much lower price floors than those with beanie hats, which are the rarest attribute…Some attributes gain market momentum randomly; for instances, the market for punks wearing hoodies has been particularly hot [during select times of the year]." Further on in his article, Matney quotes developer Max Orgeldinger who notes that while the CryptoPunk market is speculative just as the stock market is, he feels that the speculation of the CryptoPunk market is far more accurate, an assertion he justifies by noting, "With the whole NFT community, it's almost more honest because no one's getting tricked into thinking there's some very complicated math that no one can figure out. This is just people making up prices and if you want to buy it, that's the price and if you don't want to pay it, that's not the price." Interestingly, Orgeldinger points out a key difference between the stock market and the NFT market: simple valuation. When one looks at the simplicity of the NFT market, it almost becomes unjustified to compare the stock market and the NFT market, since the NFT market operates more like selling antiques at a flea market instead of selling fiscal representations of tangible assets.

As the CryptoPunks continue to attract more attention, the assertions of their being the first NFTs continue to be among the greatest controversies in the NFT environment. Even today, while many consider the CryptoPunks to be the first NFT ever created, this is largely due to their success but is not accurate. When the CryptoPunks saga began to threaten the validity of what many considered to be the true NFTs, a new position within the cryptographic world was created. Just as self-declared crypto-experts had been respected enough to assess a CryptoPunk image and declare its value based on unique characteristics, there began a new position of self-declared crypto archaeologists who were tasked with ensuring that NFTs that predated the rise of the CryptoPunks were discovered and brought to the attention of the world. In doing this, many were discovered but only one would be verified as existing prior to the release of the CryptoPunks. Even so, it was enough to dispel the rumors that the CryptoPunks were the first NFT. What can be said, however, is that the CryptoPunks were the first NFTs to reach marked success against the other digital assets.

One NFT that was introduced prior to CryptoPunks was a project known as Etheria. Built on the Ethereum platform, Etheria consisted of a map in which the users could purchase hexagonal divisions of the land. In its first days of existence, very little traction had been gained and the developers actually left the project to go pursue viable careers. When CryptoPunks began gaining attention in early 2017, the developers realized that the shortage of available punks could provide extremely valuable and thus began a new adventure for the developers: attempts to log into the old account without running out of passcode attempts. After successfully getting back into the account and confirming that the program was still operational, the developers used Twitter to announce the availability of their platform and enjoyed watching their crypto wallet balloon from being worth nothing to nearly $1.5 million in Ethereum. Just from this, it is easy to see the new landscape that has been created simply because of the creativity and persistence of the developers of CryptoPunks.

Interestingly, the ownership of the original 10,000 punks has largely stayed within the wallets of individuals who own multiple punks. Only 1,889 cyber wallets contain the CryptoPunks, giving many investors confidence that their punks will only continue to maintain or climb in value due to the limited number of wallets that currently hold the NFTs. As for the developers who originally created the CryptoPunks, they have focused their efforts now on creating more NFTs. Though none will grow in wealth or fame as their CryptoPunks have, the recognition of the CryptoPunks being among the first NFT's is reward enough for their effort. Among the projects that spun off of CryptoPunks was the famed CryptoKitties. To gain a greater understanding of how CryptoPunks inspired CryptoKitties while also seeing the contributions of the CryptoKitties, a closer look should be taken into these digitally-generated felines.

The Development of the CryptoKitties

In 2017, the landscape of NFTs had changed, with companies hopping onto the NFT market bandwagon with one goal in mind: the monetization of human habit. One of these habits was recognized by developers who postulated that if they could link the attraction and habits of mobile games to the NFT market, they could make a fortune. Fortunately for them, they were correct. In response to the success of CryptoPunks, developers at Axiom Zen launched a NFT known as CryptoKitties on the Ethereum network and waited for the funds to roll in as the game gathered more users and attracted the single-most valuable factor for long-term NFT success: replication without duplication. Whereas the CryptoPunk market focused on the scarcity of the product and secured a virtually endless appreciation of the digital assets as long as the NFT market thrived, the CryptoKitties' market focused on the replication of the digital assets while ensuring that the security of each "Kitty" was maintained and that the unique nature of each digital asset was not lost.

In replicating the CryptoKitties, the developers initiated another unique aspect and made each Kitty able to be replicated through "breeding" different Kitties. Officially, the Kitties are able to be replicated using the process of sire but this process requires the permission of both owners of the Kitties. It is here that CryptoKitties must be distinguished from the other crypto art in that it does not use the typical blockchain security but rather uses a security filter built by Axiom Zen.

The first CryptoKitties were made available in 2017 during a hackathon at the ETH Waterloo. Even as the crypto art is not secured using blockchain, the first Kitty is referred to as the Genesis and was sold for nearly $120,000 USD on the first days of its availability. To secure the Kitties against unsecured replication or duplication, the Kitties are all outfitted with a 256-bit genome that is distinctive to each cat. Additionally, the CryptoKitties followed in the footsteps of the CryptoPunks by ensuring that each Kitty has a distinguishing and unique feature. Going further then CryptoPunks, however, these distinguishable features operate as genes would in live cats and are able to be passed on to future generations of the CryptoKitties. In all, there are twelve variations of features that can be used to differentiate the Kitties.

In less than five months after the genesis Kitty was unveiled, CryptoKitties had grown so fast that it was considered sustainable on its own and Axiom Zen utilized a spinoff to create a new company called Dapper Labs, a company that would be solely dedicated to the success of the CryptoKitties. In preparing for the spinoff, a round of investing was held and nearly $12 million was net for the creation of the new laboratory. With the new CryptoKitties laboratory created, the game and crypto art has continued to grow beyond what many thought possible.

The Survival of the CryptoKitties

Since their inception in 2017, CryptoKitties have become the latest NFT fad to continue its existence as a mobile game. CryptoKitties made national headlines in 2018 when one of the Kitties netted $140,000 in a sale. Later in the same month, CryptoKitties took another page out of the CyberPunk book of success and began creating CryptoKitties that bore the likeness of celebrities. The first CryptoKittye to bear this honor would be one fashioned after Stephen Curry, the basketball legend from the Golden State Warriors. This development would prove to threaten the future of CryptoKitties after the licensing agreement between Curry and CryptoKitties was suspended due to alleged negligence of contractual obligations by Stephen Curry. What appeared to be a set back soon turned into a dramatic mess when CryptoKitties became the center of a lawsuit that alleged CryptoKitties had stolen a trade secret that was owned by Stephen Curry. Essentially, the lawsuit laid out the timeline of events during the disastrous relationship between Curry and CryptoKitties, alleging that it had actually been Stephen Curry who had approached CryptoKitties with the idea to create a CryptoKittie in his likeness. At the conclusion of the lawsuit, the judge ruled that the Dapper Labs had actually created the idea first, not Stephen Curry.

With the idea of celebrity CryptoKitties tabled for the meantime, CryptoKitties turned to a major milestone in the success of the company. After one year of existence, Dapper Labs celebrated a pool of one million cats that had been securely replicated since the inception of the genesis Kitty one year earlier. This celebration led to a subsequent round of funding, this time Dapper Labs holding a Series A round of funding in which 18 investors pledged an additional $15 million in valuation. Included in this investment round were names such as Union Square Investors, Venrock, and HOF Capital.

The arrival of the CryptoKitties took the Ethereum platform by storm, leading to some predictions that if changes were not made, CryptoKitties could severely damage the Ethereum platform. When looked at more closely, it was revealed the delays the Ethereum system were being caused by the pending transactions that had amassed to a level comprising nearly 10% of the total traffic on the Ethereum network. It was here that the proponents of crypto had a choice to make: would they allow the CryptoKitties the continued use of the system, knowing that their focus on deregulation could spell the demise of the system or would they deviate from their age-long deregulation and enact new rules. After considering the choices, a third choice was revealed that sought to both improve the Ethereum network connectivity while also retaining the deregulation. In the future, it was decided that the Ethereum miners would give additional data for each block that would then allow for more transactions per second and hopefully mitigate the risk of diminished performance. An additional measure used to speed up the network was the creation of more websites as marketplaces for the Ethereum currency. Due to the activity of the CryptoKitties, websites such as OpenSea, RareBits, and Ethertulips were created. As will be seen later, OpenSea would become the most successful out of this list of prestigious websites to come about simply due to the legendary reception of the CryptoKitties.

In November 2018, after the Series A round of funding, Axiom Zen, who was still producing the CryptoKitties as the world awaited the formulation of Dapper Labs, ceased from their previous practice of releasing a new CryptoKitty on a fifteen-minute frequency. Today, the supply of CryptoKitties is solely determined by the current owners of CryptoKitties and their ability or desire to breed their CryptoKitties. Additionally, there are means by which other owners of CryptoKitties can pay to have their CryptoKitty breed the CryptoKitty owned by a different user. Even so, the value of CryptoKitties continues to hemorrhage around $65USD per CryptoKittie, with the rare Kitties being sold for over $300,000USD. While the CryptoKitties rage continues to press onward, the focus of the NFT market has turned towards other forms of digital art and beyond the realm of mobile games.

The Individuality of CryptoKitties

What has made the CryptoKitties movement so popular is that there is an obvious means of returning value and making money vested directly in the purchase of a CryptoKitty. Whereas other NFTs require waiting for the crypto-embedded asset to appreciate in value, one could feasibly purchase a CryptoKitty, breed it with other Kitty via the sire method or the owner could even purchase another CryptoKitty and breed new Kitties at will. After this, the owner is free to list these kitties for sale, the average value being around $65-70 with more appreciable potential vested in cats with more unique features. Today, not only are people playing the mobile game: there are individuals dedicated to the long-term success of the CryptoKitties by simply breeding their cats every day.

Perhaps another element is at play in the extreme popularity of the CryptoKitties, however. Consider the adrenaline rush or even sense of belonging that occurs when a community is able to create a firestorm that raged so heavy that it threatened to break the system. As more and more users realize they are a part of something much bigger than themselves, something that is being noticed by the world, they have more of a drive to either continue contributing or to gather others to join them. Analysts have attributed this mentality and behavior to being the primary fuel behind the CryptoKitties' overtaking of the Ethereum network. In one case, the pending transaction queue rose from a daily average of 1,500 to over 11,000 transactions. Even as users were faced with unbelievably high fees per transaction and saw their purchases taking hours to complete, they maintained their interest and dedication in the network. Such is the habit of much more than loyal or simply interested individuals: such is the habits of members of a tribe.

While the average price of a CryptoKitty has fallen due to the replication factor of the Kitties, the CryptoKitties remain one of the more popular entities within the NFT network.

The Explosion of the Non-Fungible Token Infrastructure

While names such as CryptoKitties and CryptoPunks and even Colored Coins have become synonymous with the development of the NFT network, the true explosion and acceptance of the NFT system was delayed until 2018. Whereas there had been a few projects that were created sequentially, the success of one garnering the interest and subsequent success of another, the number of projects being deployed has reached a maddening fury and today, medium.com, a leading resource on the NFT market, has announced that there are over 100 projects fueled by the Ethereum and Bitcoin markets today. The two most popular NFT marketplaces today are OpenSea and SuperRare have gone beyond simply offering NFTs and now offer educational courses on how to create NFTs and what makes NFTs so important to the market today. While the success of the CryptoKitties and CryptoPunks of the market have fueled the interest in NFTs, the explosion of the NFT market is directly attributable to the efforts of OpenSea and Dapper Labs who have both made NFTs more accessible than ever before while also helping brand new developers understand the difference between successful and failing NFTs.

In 2018, as the CryptoKitty rage was beginning to wane, another rage took its place and once again, the rage centered on digitally-mastered felines. The new technology was officially referred to as "layer two" games. Essentially, these are games that rested atop the already-developed games such as CryptoKitties. What this did was allow developers the opportunity to create games that used the characters and entities of the CryptoKitties while avoiding having to build that gamification directly within the application. The new "layer two" games started somewhat of a universe or ecosystem around specific games, the most popular being the KittyVerse, which obviously centered on applications using the CryptoKitties. Within the KittyVerse, games such as KittyRace, KittyHat, and WrappedKitties fed off of the pre-existent framework and fans of the CryptoKitty environment. For CryptoKitties, the imagination of the KittyVerse breathed new life into a platform that was waning due to rapid exposure. For KittyVerse, CryptoKitties offered the benefit of not having to spend large amounts of money attempting to attract customers. With a symbiotic relationship in place, KittyVerse and CryptoKitties offered the world an example of a relationship that could prove pivotal in the future of the NFT industry.

Looking back on the history of NFTs, it is easy to see that the year 2018 offered the greatest amount of expansion within the NFT marketplace to date. Even as NFTs have continued to grow in average value and their accessibility has only gotten less limiting, the sheer growth within 2018 provided a velocity that will be hard to match. Shortly after the advent of the KittyVerse, a new craze overtook the NFT marketplace: CryptoCelebrities. Under this mechanism, the users sought out rare NFTs and purchased them. Once purchased, this NFT has its ownership transferred to the new user and is then made available for purchase once again, only to be purchased again if it is indeed rare enough. In each iteration of the sale, the subsequent selling price is a consistent percentage of the previous selling price. By doing this, the NFT is consistently appreciating in value until it reaches a point that the users find to be its fair valuation. For users fortunate enough to purchase the NFT and then sell it successfully, the difference in purchase and selling price is pocketed as profit; however, should the NFT fail to sell due to reaching its fair valuation, the new owner of the NFT is stuck hanging on to an NFT that is inherently not able to be sold until there is a change in the market, thus incurring the stock market equivalent of a loss. In fact, the whole practice resembles trading options in that the owner of the NFT is betting on the appreciation of the NFT in order to make a profit. The CryptoCelebrities took off like a wild fire, the potential for getting quick profits fueling its quick ascension. Because the NFT market was accessible by anyone, it became the haven of impulse buyers, those who thought that a particular NFT had the characteristics of a rare NFT and therefore had to be purchased before someone else did. With CryptoCelebrities dwindling from the market, there is discussion over whether their existence aided the NFT movement or injured it due to the risky bets individuals placed on their NFTs. While the NFT market remains divided over this issue, another element of the NFT was discovered and exploited through the CryptoCelebrities: the addiction of risky transactions in hopes of making profits.

Today, the NFT marketplace is operated by OpenSea, OpenBazaar, RareBits, Auctionity, Opskins, KnownOrigin.io, and moon market while the NFT infrastructure is ruled by names such as BitCrystals, tokens, Spheroid Universe, and Decentraland. While studios such as Fuel Games, Dapper Labs, Horizon and PlayStakes produce content that is fueled by the cyryptomarkets, the true facilitators of interest in the cryptomarket continue to be the games such as CryptoBaseball, CyptoKitties, Dyverse, and EtherKingdoms. Today, CryptoKitties, OxiUniverse, My Crypto Heroes, Decentraland, and Axie Infinity remain the highest performers within the mobile gaming applications for the cyryptomarkets.

Today, the NFT market remains dominated by the mobile gaming application use cases but other use cases such as virtual land ownership, event tickets, and virtual clothing are creeping into the market share of the crypto market. While the focus in the past has been on creating applications to utilize the blockchain security, today the focus is shifting towards creating interoperability. For a truly deregulated system to completely usable, the assets must be interoperable between different applications and fortunately, that is becoming a reality. Though still in testing, the future of NFTs truly remains beyond current vision. While the future is difficult to imagine, the past is enjoyable to look back on, the genius and creativity of the developers teaming up with the deregulated and decentralized system where anyone can be a winner, provided they provide content that is accepted by the crypto-society. If the past five years is any indication, the NFT market will continue to rapidly evolve and perhaps begin challenging stalwarts of society such as tangible currency. Only the future knows.

The Future of Non-Fungible Tokens

While CryptoKitties, CryptoCelebrities, and the KittyVerse gave non-fungible tokens world exposure, their rapid expansion caused some holes to develop in the NFT infrastructure, holes that needed to be fixed with patience. As the rage from these fads rolled on, it was difficult for NFT developers to spend their time working on fixing the holes when other developers less dedicated to the future of NFTs were more focused on making profits. In time, however, as the excitement surrounding the NFT market wore off, the developers and their labs refocused on creating a sustainable environment. As the market of less-dedicated users continued to dwindle, the developers turned their attention to the loyal users and their immediate needs. As the dust settled, the NFT world turned their attention from the gaming platforms and began focusing on digital assets. While the NFT market had been primarily focused on gaming platforms, digital art platforms began to gather show interest, developers SuperRare, Rare Art Labs, MakersPlace, and KnownOrigin giving artists platforms where they could create digital art and infuse NFTs to ensure security and ownership. Over time, digital art became known as crypto art, forums such as Cent opening their doors to artists.

As the focus gradually turned away from mobile gaming platforms, it also became evident that a market existed for individuals who had no development experience. Whereas previous deployments required that a developer fashion a smart contract, Digital Art Chain was born out of a desire that anyone be able to create an NFT, regardless of programming ability. All the users had to do was upload a digital image and an NFT token was minted. Later that year, a deviation of Digital Art Chain known as Marble Cards was created, this time users being able to input a URL into the Marble Cards engine. After doing so, a unique image would be created from the contents of the URL and an accompanying NFT would be minted. Of the NFT software products created during this phase, Marble Cards would be the most controversial by far.

As NFT-generating engines became the new fad, other software projects such as Mintbase and Mintable became very popular. These minting machines were created to operate within web browsers, giving individuals even more access to being able to create their own NFTs. For users focused primarily on the creation of trading cards or tickets, The Kred offers users a streamlined version of an NFT generator. Kred would gain further national attention when it joined teams with CoinDesk in the creation of a virtual, digital version of a "Swag Bag" that was given to all who attended the Consensus Conference. Today, the most popular NFT marketplace continues to be OpenSea, due to the ease with which users can create and sell NFTs on their marketplace.

Today, the development of NFT generators has both created more interest in the market while also lowering the costs associated with creating NFTs. Large organizations have shown their interest in also joining the NFT craze, the Major League Baseball Association signing a contract with Lucid Sight to bring about a baseball card trading game on the NFT platform. Not to be outdone, Formula1 Racing also joined the hype with the F1DeltaTime, a game that allows users to amass F1DeltaTime's currency Revv. In addition to the NFT generators, the greatest development of the latest phase in the history of NFTs has been the globalization of the NFT market. The internet has allowed countries to join in the creation of NFTs together and Japan has thus proven to be among the leaders in producing NFTs.

Briefly mentioned earlier, another development within the NFT marketplace has been the birth of trading card games. One example of this is Magic the Gathering, a trading card game that quickly grew to be more than a game—it became a culture. Today, the ecosystem of the trading card atmosphere is reaching CryptoKitty levels of hype, with multiple websites being put up simply to educate users on the value of certain trading cards. Another famous trading card game on the NFT marketplace is Gods Unchained, founded by Immutable. Fueled by a political stance, Gods Unchained quickly grew to become a stalwart of the blockchain movement, amassing over $1.3 million in the first offering of the cards.

Along with the trading cards, major corporations are starting to realize the functionality of NFTs, one of the more notable corporations being Microsoft. To support their contributors on their website, Microsoft developed the Azure Heroes, a series of badges that are rare enough to be a hot commodity on for developers within the Azure community. Not only are corporations interested in the capabilities of the NFTs: so are the governments. Recently, the Australian Postal Service jumped on board the NFT train with Crypto Stamp, a tangible stamp with Ethereum influence. Under Crypto Stamp, individuals who purchased a tangible stamp were able to scratch off a portion of the stamp, revealing a private key that was linked to a small portion of Ether. Additionally, the stamp held a key that was linked to an NFT, which could then be sold. To date, this marked the first time that an NFT could be purchased with a tangible item such as a stamp. The move proved to be genius, however, igniting hopes that the once forgotten hobby of stamp collecting might have new life breathed into it.

One last development within the NFT marketplace that is worth mentioning is the asset of domain names. Following the edicts of the decentralization and deregulation, NFTs are now able to launch domain names, which can be purchased using Ethereum. This is made possible through the Ethereum Name Service, which quickly sold so many domain names that it held nearly 170,000 ETH in exchange for the domain names. Today, the Ethereum Name Service has developed its abilities to include the ERC721 standard that will be mentioned later. In short, the ERC721 standard allows the domain name to be sold and purchased on multiple platforms, essentially offering interoperability. As the naming services sector of the NFT industry has recently begun to grow, venture capitalists have become highly interested in the profit potential of this sector. Most notably, venture capitalists rushed to fund Unstoppable Domains, a naming system that garnered nearly $4 million in a Series A rounding of investment. Today, websites can be accessed using the .crypto suffix. Future implementations of this technology hope to link DNS services with the ENS services, thus making it possible to link digital wallets and websites.

The Basics of the Non-Fungible Tokens

While the history of the non-fungible tokens is exciting and inspiring, delving into how the non-fungible tokens are comprised will take the reader on a journey of fascination and most likely, confusion. In its most basic state, a non-fungible token (NFT) is the certification that one person is the sole owner of a digital object. In addition to certifying ownership, the NFT certifies the authenticity of that particular digital asset. These digital assets can vary in shape, form, or size but the most frequent digital assets are GIFs, memes, or digital art. In reality, non-fungible tokens can actually take on the form of anything that is unique. Provided an asset is not "able to be replaced by another identical item," it qualifies as an NFT.

What makes an NFT so appealing to creators of digital art is that in the past, there was no way to secure digital art once it was published on a digital medium. Today, however, the original piece of that digital art is verifiable through the use of checking its validity through an NFT. While non-fungible tokens do not do anything to cease the replication or distribution of these digital assets, the non-fungible tokens do verify whether a digital asset is the original or whether it is a reproduction. By this means, digital assets are able to be sold and purchased. While this idea may seem a bit far-fetched to some, it is beginning to gain traction and saw some high-profile cases in 2021. Such was the case when Beeple, a digital artist, sole one of his works through the use of a NFT, the selling price coming to nearly $70 million USD. Later that same year, Jack Dorsey, the founder of the popular social media site, sold the rights to his first tweet from 2006, netting nearly $3 million USD, all of which he donated to charity. While it may be mind-boggling to see the market exploding with digital assets that were once never even thought sellable, it is also the perfect time for one to become involved in the NFT market. Simply looking at the price of Bitcoin or Ether over the past few years gives enough context around the assertion that any crypto market is volatile at best. With prices high right now, non-fungible tokens are being sold quickly and present a great opportunity for digital artists.

In regards to the understanding that the cryptomarkets are volatile, one might be concerned with the future of NFTs and whether investing a large amount of capital in the production of NFTs is a bad choice destined to be a capital loss. With that in mind, consider that the growth of the NFT market is a relatively recent development but an important one considering the recent trend among companies to digitize their environment. In a world moving quickly towards new levels of digitization, it would appear that NFTs are well-positioned to aid in the digitization of the business environment. Additionally, NFTs allow for the globalization of art distribution, giving even more credence to the development of this technology.

As NFTs are looked at more closely, there should be distinction made between digital assets and non-fungible tokens. Digital assets are usually constructed for a single environment and are therefore unable to be interchanged between different platforms. A great way to demonstrate this would be someone attempting to sell an award earned in a mobile application on eBay or Amazon. It can be done but it is extremely difficult and there is a good bit of faith that is placed in the seller in regards to the validity of the exchange. This is primarily due to the difference in standards across the digital environment. With this lack of unity in regards to the standards, assets have been constrained to their respective industry and in some cases, companies or originators. This lack of unity could be thought of as if countries all had their own currency but no market for currency exchange existed. In the event of digital assets, non-fungible tokens act as that currency exchange, allowing assets to take on any shape and simply be represented by the "title and deed" of that asset, the blockchain NFT.

Today, the different blockchain protocols all have different standards regarding how much data they will be requiring but the commonalities include ownership, simple access control, and standards of transfer. Devin Finzer, CEO and founder of the popular OpenSea NFT marketplace, describes blockchain as "a layer on top that gives developers a brand new set of stateful primitives on which to build applications." With the industry standardized by ownership but not form of asset, NFTs have transitioned from being constrained to developer wallets to being able to operate across different platforms. Additionally, as Finzer goes on to point out in his article, NFTs create a higher level of liquidity among the stakeholders willing to invest in the volatile markets.

To gain a greater understanding of how these NFTs are able to operate across different systems and platforms, it is helpful to look at the token standards that provide the security that makes NFTs so appealing. The definition of these standards is "the guarantee that assets will behave in a specific way [while outlining] how to interact with the basic functionality of the assets." There are numerous token standards and this guide will attempt to bring the most pertinent and useful token to light.

The Token Standards of NFTs

Piloted by the raging CryptoKitties of the 2017-2018 era of NFTs, ERC721 is a set of digits that represents the standard used for outlining the behavior of the CryptoKitty NFTs. Readers will recall the unique means of replication that were outlined by Axiom Zion and later Dapper Labs; that means of replication is stored within ERC721 and ensures that each user and owner of the CryptoKitties has equal opportunity and access for the full availability of the CryptoKitties. The ERC721 token is defined as a "solidity smart contract standard" with the purpose of allowing developers the opportunity to replicate ERC721 contracts within their respective ecosystems through the OpenZeppelin library. To create an ERC721 contract, developers simply create or copy and paste code from other developers such as GitHub. The contracts all contain a line of code that is inherited from a previous contract that is fostered within the OpenZeppelin ERC721 contracts. An additional component that can be added to the ERC721 smart contracts is an act known as whitelisting, which will allow any users of a particular platform to trade items within that platform gas-free. To avoid confusion, recall that when in the context of cryptography, gas refers to "fee or pricing value that is required to successfully conduct a transaction or execute a contract on the Ethereum blockchain platform."

After choosing to whitelist or not, the developer will the begin the process of deploying the newly formed smart contract. This can easily be done by using an application program interface, also known as an API. While certain

APIs require financial backing through cryptocurrencies, others are free and simply require the use of "seed words." After the contract is deployed, the developer can begin possibly the most exciting portion of the development journey: minting the tokens or currency. These tokens will be minted into a separate account that is controlled by the developer and will become the exchange of sorts for either USD to the currency or for the representation of a tangible asset. While this process may seem easy, the contracts can range in complexity, with some taking only ten minutes to complete while others take days or even months to complete. With the smart contract complete, the ERC721 standard is created and the developer is able to begin making financial gains on his newly secured contract.

While the ERC721 was made famous by means of the CryptoKitties, it is hardly the only token standard. Another well-known token standard is the ERC1155, which was brought into existence by a development team known as Enjin Team. The ERC1155 is not the same as the ERC721 in more than one respect but the greatest difference lies in how the two protocols regard assets. While the ERC721 considers an asset an individual entity, the ERC1155 is a protocol designed for classes of assets. In their explanation of the ERC1155 token standard, OpenSea described it as follows: "For instance, an ID might represent 'swords' and a wallet could own 1,000 of these swords. In this case, the balanceOf method would return the number of swords owned by a wallet and a user can transfer any number of these swords by calling transferFrom with the 'sword' ID." As is later pointed out, the primary draw of the ERC1155 token standard over the ERC721 is that the developers can be far more efficient in their creation of the contracts. Returning to OpenSea's example of the sword contract, should someone want a set number of the swords, they could simply transfer that amount with no problem. Were the individual to be using the ERC721 protocol, however, such a transfer would require editing numerous portions of the smart contract.

Even as the ERC1155 protocol offers greater efficiency, some diehard blockchain supporters rush to point out that this deviation in standard reduces the amount of information that is contained within any one transaction. Whereas ERC721 contracts are able to trace the ownership over every single asset, the information would be bound in the smart contract of the collection of assets for those using the ERC1155 token standard and would therefore be less concise. Today, the ERC1155 continues to overtake the ERC721 as the preferred token standard.

An additional token standard that is used today is the ERC-20 standard. This standard is deigned as "…having its own specific utility, such as granting users the right to vote on decisions impacting the future of a project, or rewarding customers for performing certain tasks." Following in the footsteps of the other token standards, the ERC-20 is held in check by the smart contracts included in the NFT. This smart contract houses the rules that will ensure the token operates as intended, regardless of its ownership. The three primary elements that are required when using the ERC-20 token standard are totalSupply, balanceOf, and transfer.

One Token Standard to Rule Them All

With the three standards outlined above referring to the token standards of non-fungible tokens, it can be easy to forget that fungible assets do exist and are still a part of the cryptographic world. To review, while non-fungible tokens are assets that are not able to be replaced equally or evenly, fungible tokens are able to be replaced with an asset that is completely equal. For example, there is nothing unique about one Bitcoin. It can be replaced evenly and with a different Bitcoin, thus rendering it a fungible token. With this in mind, concerns could be raised over how securing a transaction involving both non-fungible and fungible assets can be increased. This is able to be accomplished by using templates provided by a series of NFT's known as composable. According to medium.com, composables are defined as "A standard extension for any non-fungible token (NFT) to own another non-fungible ERC-721 token or fungible ERC-20 tokens." Within composables, digital assets are able to also "pass on" aspects of the previous generation, in a sense giving a single entity a series of reoccurring features that are unique to that smart contract. Today, this market of composables is secured by the token standard ERC-998, which allows the concurrent ownership of non-fungible and fungible assets. This standard is actually somewhat exemplified in the existence of the CryptoKitties who are able to pass along certain "genes" to future generations of their own Kitties. To date, this is one of the only examples of composables but nonetheless provides developers with yet another resource should their creative genius take them on the path less traveled.

The Composition of Non-Fungible Tokens

With the understanding that the non-fungible tokens are given life through the existence of a smart contract and an accompanying token standard, it is time to take a look at what truly comprises the NFT, the heartbeat of the NFT. When one considers how the Earth is composed, all elements breaking down into the smallest known form of matter known as the atom, consider the atom of the cryptography environment to be the metadata. When one comes across a smart contract that they would like more information about, there are means by which the ownership and composition of the digital asset can be discovered.

To discover the owner of a smart contract, one would only need to use the ownerOf method on a crypto marketplace. Doing so would show the wallet address of the owner along with the current owner. To go further and see what the owner of a specific smart contract truly owns, one would need to consult the metadata of that particular smart contract. As defined, metadata is essentially the description of what that particular digital asset looks like. In addition to telling the name of that particular asset, there could be a link to an image of this asset and a brief synopsis of what the digital asset truly is.

When developers are looking into the creation of the metadata for a particular digital asset, there are two means by which this data can be referenced. The first is known as on-chain metadata and is quite self-explanatory. When a developer uses on-chain metadata, they develop the metadata directly into the digital asset. This provides numerous conveniences to the owner, above all that the information regarding this digital asset will always be included with the NFT. Additionally, hosting the metadata directly within the NFT allows for easy updates should the NFT be replicated. This is easily understood when considered in the context of the CryptoKitties where Kitties are being created every day, each bearing some resemblance to the parent asset. During the creation of the new CryptoKitty, the on-chain metadata is referenced.

Even as the convenience of on-chain metadata is seen, it is easily superseded in usage by its counterpart, off-chain metadata. This is due to one constraint that has become well-known to users of Ethereum: the data storage limits. One would recall that in the first days of CryptoKitties, the Ethereum marketplace became so slow that its existence was threatened. The same threat posed by the CryptoKitties is posed by excess on-chain metadata giving developers all the more reason to opt for off-chain metadata. To ensure that the metadata for the NFT is accessible, the token standards include functions that allow for the identification of a location specified by the developer as being the resting place of the metadata. Developers choosing to use off-chain metadata storage solutions are able to choose one of two primary storage locations. The first, centralized servers, allows for the developers to store the metadata in an easily accessible location that is also recognized by the majority of developers. Leading solutions include

Amazon Web Services. While the centralized services offer a cost-effective means of storing the metadata, some owners are scared off by the threat that the developer could change the metadata without the consent or knowledge of the new owner. Additionally, there is the threat of data loss, a threat that is somewhat mitigated by the Ethereum marketplaces that host cached metadata to ensure a reliable backup.

The alternative to using centralized servers as a data storage solution is the InterPlanetary File System, also referred to as the IPFS. When considered in comparison with the edicts of the blockchain and Ethereum standards, the IPFS resembles more than simply an off-site data storage solution. Not only is the IPFS decentralized, it is also operated on a peer-to-peer network so that the storage and replication of files across the network is not hampered by risk of data loss from a server crash. With the protection of the nodes, the metadata stored in the IPFS is secure for what many would assert, forever. Today, the IPFS remains the most used alternative to storing the metadata on-chain.

With an understanding of the composition of the NFTs, it might be helpful to end this guide by relaying the steps needed to create an NFT. With their exposure growing daily, understanding how to create an NFT could be a great side job or even turn into a career in the near future.

Creating a Non-Fungible Token

With the explosion of the NFT industry, creating them has become easier each year. When done correctly and with intuition, creating NFTs can prove to be a valuable art. To begin the process, developers of NFTs must decide which blockchain they will be using. While Ethereum remains the most popular blockchain service, it is not perfect and other blockchains such as Binance Smart Coin, Tron, Polkadot, or Tezos are a few of the leading names that compete with Ethereum. When choosing which blockchain service to utilize, it is important to remember that the choice of blockchain will guide the token standard and marketplace of this NFT. Therefore, the choice of which blockchain to use should be made carefully.

After choosing which blockchain service to use, the developers will need to comply with the standards of the marketplace associated with that blockchain. For instance, were one to use the Ethereum blockchain, they would need to find a wallet that was compatible with Ethereum and then the token standard of Ethereum based blockchains: ERC721. Following their choice of wallet, the developer will then need to transfer funding so that they have adequate currency in ether.

Following the transfer of funding, the most exciting stage of creating an NFT commences: the choice of which platform to use. If using Ethereum, the developer will be able to choose from the widest array of marketplaces for the NFT, the largest being OpenSea followed by Variable and Mintable.

Each marketplace will have its own standards for uploading an NFT but most developers collectively agree that the OpenSea marketplace is the easiest to use. When uploading an NFT to OpenSea, the first step is to connect the pre-established crypto wallet to OpenSea. Once completed, the process of uploading the NFT becomes as easy as adding pictures to social media. The developer will upload a separate image of what defines the "collection" of NFTs. This would be similar to the profile picture of a leading social media site while the accompanying "banner" image also resembles the cover photo of a popular social media site. To add the specific NFT, the user can continue with the process of uploading the NFT, each site hosting its own practice for uploading.

One would recall that what differentiates NFTs and drives up their value is the rarity or unique features. To ensure that an NFT is awarded for all of its unique features, most marketplaces will also allow the user the chance to specify what unique traits should be considered when qualifying the value of the NFT. After outlining what specifically makes this NFT so unique, the user can then add the NFT to their collection and the process for adding an NFT is complete until someone purchases the NFT. Just from this brief overview, one can see that the process of creating NFTs has become extremely easy and cost-effective. Today, the highest cost in selling NFTs is either the time that the creator needed to create the NFT and an additional fee when the NFT is sold. For those selling their NFTs on the Ethereum blockchain platforms, the cost is referred to as "gas." This price is variable and directly correlates with the number of users on the network. Doing so allows for self-regulation while also driving up the price of NFTs that were submitted at high-volume moments.

An additional means of creating a value stream is through royalties. By pricing NFTs lower than the market standard but adding in a royalty to be paid every time the NFT changes ownership, a developer can actually glean more from the sale of their NFT. Based on the growth of the NFT market in just the past five years, the future for NFTs looks very promising. While it can be estimated that drivers such as bitcoin and ether will keep the interest in the crypto market peaked, one can only begin to imagine what the future versions of the NFTs will be. In a recent sale, billionaire Mark Cuban sold an NFT with one of his famous quotes. The quote sums up the history and future of the NFT environment perfectly: "Nobody ever changed the world by doing what everyone else was doing." For the NFT industry, it always has been and always will be about doing what is different. Only then do the rules of scarcity drive the valuation of NFTs and only then does the future of NFTs look as bright as it does now.

Printed in Great Britain
by Amazon